Maximize Your Competitive Edge:
17 Secrets to Make Your Small Business Look Like a Fortune 500 Company

Carol J. Amato

STARGAZER
Publishing Company
PO Box 77002
Corona, CA 92877-0100

"Educate, Enlighten, Entertain"

www.stargazerpub.com

STARGAZER
QUICK
GUIDES

Published by Stargazer Publishing Company
PO Box 77002
Corona, CA 92877-0001
(800) 606-7895
(951) 898-4619
FAX (951) 898-4633
e-mail: stargazer@stargazerpub.com
website: http://www.stargazerpub.com

Cover Design: www.calypso.concepts.com

ISBN: 9781933277158 (trade paper)
9781933277165 (Kindle)
9781933277172 (e-pub)

Library of Congress Cataloging-in-Publication Data

Amato, Carol J.
    Maximize your competitive edge : 17 secrets to make your small
    business look like a fortune 500 company / Carol J. Amato.
        p. cm. -- (Stargazer quick guides)
    Includes bibliographical references.
    ISBN 978-1-933277-15-8 (trade pbk.) -- ISBN 978-1-933277-16-5
    (kindle ed.) -- ISBN 978-1-933277-17-2 (e-pub ed.)
    1. Small business--Management. 2. Strategic planning. I. Title.
    HD62.7.A485 2012
    658.02'2--dc23

                                                2012034167

Other Books by Carol J. Amato

Maximize Your Visibility: Exhibiting at Trade Shows on a Shoestring Budget (2015)

Forerunner (2015)

The Phantom Hunters: The Secret of Blackhurst Manor (2015)

The World's Easiest Guide to Using the APA, 5th Edition, (2014)

The World's Easiest Guide to Using the MLA, 2nd Edition, (2014)

The 5 Biggest Writing Mistakes Small Business Owners Make and How to Avoid them

Writing Cool Short Stories

Writing Cool Short Stories Workbook

Writing Cool Short Stories Teacher's Guide

Running a Writers' Critique Group in Your Classroom

The World's Easiest Guide to Using the APA, 4th Edition

How to Start and Run a Writers' Critique Group

The Phantom Hunters: The Lost Treasure of the Golden Sun Teacher's Guide

The Phantom Hunters: The Lost Treasure of the Golden Sun

Persistence is Power! A Real-World Guide for the Newly Disabled Employee

The World's Easiest Guide to Using the APA, 3rd Edition

The World's Easiest Guide to Using the MLA

The World's Easiest Guide to Using the APA, 2nd Edition

The Earth

Creepy Crawlies

The World's Easiest Guide to Using the APA

50 Nifty Super Science Fair Projects

Super Science Fair Projects

50 Nifty Science Fair Projects

Inside Out: The Wonders of Modern Technology Explained

Breakthroughs in Science: The Earth

Breakthroughs in Science: Astronomy

Breakthroughs in Science: The Human Body

Breakthroughs in Science: Inventions

What Other People Say....

"Today, more than ever, emerging businesses must become the experts in their fields and position themselves as Fortune 500 corporations to compete. Carol J. Amato's book, *Maximize Your Competitive Edge* presents simple steps to do just that. Get a copy!"

—Ursula Mentjes, President
Sales Coach Now

"Building business success just became easier with Carol Amato's new book, *Maximize Your Competitive Edge*. Carol translates what is often perceived as a complicated struggle into a simple roadmap that can lead small companies to becoming business stars— competing easily with the giants. This is a must-read!

— Diane Weklar, President
The Weklar Consulting Group

"With an ever-changing business environment and all the new businesses starting up, it is important to know the new marketing strategies while being technology-savvy. Competing for market share should be on top of your to-do list. In *Maximize Your Competitive Edge*, Carol Amato shows you, with simple steps and a clear understanding, how to answer the many questions you may have on how to achieve your goals."

— Carol Miller, President
Posh Productions, Inc.

"Simply put, *Maximize Your Competitive Edge* offers techniques about that classic art of becoming a successful business owner. You learn how to tell your story with polish. You are the storyteller, and Carol's book helps you succeed in your business communication."

— Joy Mellen White, President, Retired
Infoteam Inc.

Leading a business in our global economy can be a daunting task. *Maximize Your Competitive Edge* is a strong solution to figuring out what to do and where to start. This impressive business tool adds order and structure to growing your business infrastructure."

— Sophia Brooks, President
Global Learning Partners, Inc.

"Maximize Your Competitive Edge is a must-read for today's small business owners. Filled with up-to-date information, it covers a wide range of topics often missed in other "how-to" business books.... It's not long-winded and pedantic like so many others. Carol distills the important issues affecting small businesses to a very concise, readable and useful "handbook" that can be used over and over as a great reference to keep you on track to success. I highly recommend it!"

— *Richard Fliedner, former President,*
Adair Office Furniture, Inc.
Small Business Consultant

"Maximize Your Competitive Edge is a must read for any small business owner competing with larger well-funded organizations. The 17 steps are easy to follow and serve as an invaluable checklist for all business owners striving for a competitive advantage."

— *Nikki G. Gralnick, J.D., M.P.A.*
Director, HRM Specialists
Corporate Training and Consulting

"*Maximize Your Competitive Edge* is a no-brainer, 'go-to' reference for any small business owner or entrepreneur who wants to play big in a highly competitive marketplace. Carol has done a masterful job identifying these 17 secrets. The chapter on branding was powerful and helped me to become crystal clear about my business and how I show up in the world with purpose."

— *Gwen Chambers, SPHR*
Strategic HR Business Partner
Chambers HR Consulting Group, Inc.

"Carol has taken the 'secret' out of making your business look like a Fortune 500 company with clear and understandable strategies to set your business apart from the competition and achieve even greater success."

— *Eli Sense*
Sensewrite Communications

Dedication

To Dylan, Justin, Ashton, Mackenzie, Kyla, and Kelsey

Acknowledgements

My heartfelt thanks to my trusted critique group colleagues, whose help and advice have been invaluable throughout the process of writing this book: Amanda Ashley, Molly Dillon, Judy McAllister, Martin Shaughnessy, Maria Toth, C. Sonberg Larsen, Nancy O'Connor, Annie Howland, Lynn Kelley, Marissa Perez, Joanna Woods, Kathy Sant, Alanna Heck, Julie Fredericksen, Leah Leonard, Steve Attkisson, Melissa Salazar, and Tommy Kovac.

Thanks also to Great-Grampa Salvatore Amato for insisting his children emigrate from Termini Imerese, Sicily, to the United States, making it possible for me to be born in this country. Even though I never had the chance to meet you, you will always be in my heart. My biggest thanks to Grampa Calogero Salvatore (C. S.) Amato and Grampa Salvatore Dindia, who both agreed to leave Termini to start a new life in the United States, where they could succeed as entrepreneurs. Even though you both passed away too many years ago to count, I still miss you.

You and our other relatives who followed in your footsteps have provided me a long line of mentors, making the idea of successfully running my own business one that was achievable.

Maximize Your Competitive Edge

Table of Contents

Introduction

You're an entrepreneur because you like being your own boss and you know your expertise is valuable to your market. You can provide quality to your customers, and you want to live a life where you call the shots and can spend more leisure time with your friends and family. Yet, are you still asking yourself these questions?

- Why am I still struggling to break free from my competition?

- How can I be the go-to person/company in my specialization?

- Why don't my meetings with clients go as well as I hoped?

- Why do my proposals get rejected time after time without any apparent reason?

- How can I double or triple my income this year?

Small businesses are the backbone of the economy. According to the Bureau of Labor Statistics,[1] as of March, 2010, 505,473 new small businesses started up in the U. S. In this economy, however, competition is stiff. Being at the top of your industry is all the more critical to achieving the dream lifestyle you want.

Whether you're new to the world of entrepreneurship or you've been in business for years, you may be wondering just what will set you apart. You have skill, talent, and professional connections. What's missing may be some of the details you may not have considered:

- Being technology-savvy
- Branding your company
- Knowing the new marketing strategies
- Realizing the true public face of your business
- Being aware of how your clients perceive you
- Knowing what you're worth

The image that your small business projects in writing, speaking, marketing, and visual appearance can determine if a client hires you or not. Whether you work from home as a solopreneur or have a physical location with employees makes no difference. If you want your enterprise to stand apart, give it a Fortune 500 company image. *Maximize Your Competitive Edge* shows you the top 17 strategies to create ongoing success. No matter what kind of business you have, read on to discover the 17 secrets to make your business look like a Fortune 500 company and outshine your competition.

Secret #1:

Perfect Your Writing Skills

"You can have brilliant ideas, but if you can't get them across, your ideas won't get you anywhere."

— Lee Iacocca

Secret #1:
Perfect Your Writing Skills

Your writing is YOU. It is the public face of your company. Your customers and clients will judge the quality of your products or services by the quality of your written communication. Two areas are absolutely critical: grammar, punctuation, and spelling skills and using accepted document formats.

Grammar, Punctuation, and Spelling

Nothing ruins a person's credibility more than poor writing. Never let any written document go out under your name or out of your company without ensuring that everything is error-free. Edit your documents and proofread them several times by reading aloud. Ask others who are skilled at writing mechanics to read over the documents, too, or hire an editor or proofreader.

"I made the mistake of not proofreading a contract before sending it out," says Sharon Johnson, the owner of a small machinery company. "I left a zero off the price of our most expensive piece of equipment. The customer signed the contract and bought the machine for $5,000 rather than $50,000. It's a mistake I won't repeat."

Grammar

Become proficient at spotting and correcting the following:

- Sentence fragments
- Run-on sentences
- Comma splices
- Agreement problems
  - subject/verb
  - subject/pronoun
- Improper
  - pronoun forms
  - verb forms
  - verb tenses
- Misused adjectives/adverbs
- Incorrect word choice
- Redundancy/wordiness
- Passive voice
- Double negatives
- Dangling/misplaced modifiers

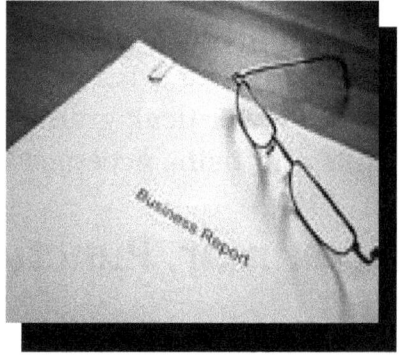

Don't rely on grammar check; it picks up mostly passive voice and skips over many grammar errors. In addition, it doesn't tell you how to correct the errors it does find.

Spelling

Read your document aloud so that you can catch any spelling mistakes. Don't use only spell-check. It is no more reliable than grammar check. It will fly right over incorrectly spelled words that still spell English words, such as "write" for "right," "your" for "you're," "four" for "for," "two" for "to" or "too," etc. There is no substitute for the human eye.

Also, avoid abbreviations such as those used in texting. They have no place in the business world if your aim is to impress.

Punctuation

Be proficient in using the following:

- commas
- apostrophes
- quotation marks
- colons
- semi-colons
- parentheses

- capitalization
- abbreviations
- numbers
- hyphens
- brackets
- ellipses

If your documents contain the errors described above, your clients may conclude that the quality of your products and services is poor. If you don't care enough to ensure the documents your own company puts out are perfect, how can clients be sure that you would do a perfect job for them?

Keep a dictionary on your desk along with a good grammar reference guide. Since the English language constantly changes, replace the dictionary every four years and the grammar reference guide every five years.

Use Accepted Document Formats

Documents that don't exhibit the standard formats look amateurish. Each type of message has its own formula. One size does not fit all. Writing the following kinds of messages in the correct manner is critical to achieving their purposes, such as:

- *good news*

  Lay it on them!

- *bad news*

  Tread carefully. No one wants to hear bad news.

- *persuasive*

  Can you convince the reader to take your side or adopt your idea?

- *argument*

  Debate both sides of an issue—pros and cons

- *informational*

  Everyone wants to be kept up-to-date.

Likewise, each format has multiple structures:

- e-mail
- letter
- report

- proposal
- manual
- ad
- brochure
- flyer
- postcard
- contract
- business plan
- marketing plan
- form

Within the report category, there are several different types, each with their own specific constructions. These include but are not limited to:

- informational
- progress/status
- recommendation
- instructional
- analytical
- situational
- feasibility
- investigative
- compliance
- yardstick
- research

Reports and proposals also have an:

• abstract

• executive summary

and a

• cover letter

Be well acquainted with the appropriate structures for all of these, the differences between an executive summary and an abstract, and how to write both. Reports of all types going outside your company need a cover letter. Know the proper formula for creating one of these, too.

Secret #2:

Develop Superior Presentation Skills

"Proper Planning and Preparation Prevents Poor Performance."

— Stephen Keague

Secret #2:
Develop Superior
Presentation Skills

Public speaking ranks as the average American's number one fear. This isn't anything new. A Tamil poet who lived over two thousand years ago, Thiruvalluvar, is attributed with saying: "Many are ready to die in battle, but few can face an assembly without nerves." Sentiments like this one have been expressed throughout history.

While today's business professional doesn't have to worry about dying in battle, the fear of speaking in front of others still exists. This fear has to be overcome if you want to be at the top of your industry.

The ability to speak well tells a lot about a person. If your small business requires you to present to clients or customers, it is essential to be articulate, intelligent, and clear. This means not only having excellent speaking abilities, but also knowing how to use PowerPoint or other visual media.

Don't rely on skills you learned in speech class. Speeches tend to be stilted and preachy and often lack audience interaction. Presentations, on the other hand, should be engaging, entertaining, and educational. The purpose is to build relationships by being conversational and interactive.

For product or instructional presentations, you can and should answer questions throughout the discussion and afterwards.

Being an excellent presenter not only increases your confidence and makes networking easier, it also increases your brand visibility (branding is covered in Secret No. 5). You can conduct workshops based on your expertise. You can be a guest speaker at local, regional, and national conferences and for local organizations, and once you have some experience behind you, you can get paid. More people will see you and your brand, and because of that visibility, clients will recognize you and pick you over others in your field.

If you have no experience at all, you may think that becoming a good presenter is an impossible challenge. Remember this quote from Dale Carnegie, author and developer of famous courses in public speaking, salesmanship, and interpersonal skills: "Great speakers are not born. They are trained." You can be trained, too.

Consider joining Toastmasters (www.toastmasters. org). This national, non-profit group helps people with no public-speaking skills to develop them through practice and feedback. It's a terrific place to start to get over those initial jitters of standing up in front of a group. Look for a chapter in your area. Keep in mind that Toastmasters offers speech training, however, not presentation training.

Another great starting point is the Dale Carnegie course, "Getting Rid of the Fear and Horror of Public Speaking" (http://www.dalecarnegie.com/events/sub ject/?F_s=6).

Once you feel comfortable presenting in front of others, polish your skills with these resources:

- ***The Ultimate Guide to Professional Speaking*** by Tom Antion (http://snipurl.com/253rpej). This terrific e-book arms you with strategies and techniques to make money from your speaking.

- ***Passionately Speaking Protégé*** program (www. instantprospeaker.com). Arvee Robinson's program consists of weekly coaching calls, a super archive of calls from the past several years (all downloadable .mp3 audio files), and an e-zine.

- ***NSA Academy for Professional Speaking*** (http://www.nsaspeaker.org/join/types-of-mem bership/aspiring-speaker#). This year-long, face-to-face and distance-learning program sponsored by the National Speakers' Association is designed to help you make the jump from being a great speaker to being a paid speaker.

- ***The Presentation Secrets of Steve Jobs*** by Carmine Gallo. ISBN: 9780071636087. With this book, you can learn from a master!

Providing visuals for your audience is also important. Some people learn by hearing (audio learners), while other people learn by seeing (visual learners).

For visual learners, hearing the presentation may not be enough. Information can go in one ear and out the other. Create PowerPoint slides to accompany your presentation. They not only benefit your audience, they also cue you if you lose your place. Add images for interest.

Still others learn by doing (hands-on learners). These people expect printed materials to take away with them. PowerPoint can create handouts for you. Check out these websites for free tutorials for beginners:

- www.homeandlearn.co.uk/powerpoint/power point.html (PowerPoint XP through 2003)

- http://presentationsoft.about.com/od/power point2010/yp/100420-learningpowerpoint 2010.htm

The following books are also very helpful:

- ***PowerPoint 2007 for Dummies***, by Doug Lowe. ISBN: 9780470040591 $24.99
  Kindle edition $9.99

- ***Microsoft Office PowerPoint 2007 Step-by-Step***, by Joyce Cox and Joan Pruppernau. ISBN: 9780735623019 $24.99
  Kindle edition $9.99

- ***Microsoft PowerPoint 2010 Plain and Simple,*** by Nancy Muir. ISBN: 9780735627284 $24.99
  Kindle edition $9.99

These resources will make your presentation skills top-notch. You'll look like an expert in no time!

Secret #3:

Be Computer Literate

"What a computer is to me is the most remarkable tool that we have ever come up with. It's the equivalent of a bicycle for our minds."

— Steve Jobs

Secret #3:
Be Computer Literate

C omputer illiteracy costs you time and money. It's not enough to expect your employees to be proficient. You need these skills yourself. The three main programs to know to at least an intermediate level are:

- Microsoft Word
- Microsoft PowerPoint
- Microsoft Excel

To develop your skills, take hands-on classes at a community college or through adult ed, or find someone who can teach you one-to-one. One-day seminars are also available through the national seminar companies www.fredpryor.com, www.skillpath.com, www.padgett-thompson.com, and www.nationseminars.com) (all owned by the same parent group), but they are useful if you are at an intermediate or advanced level, as they generally are not hands-on.

If you are good at teaching yourself, get some of the Dummies series books. You can learn at your own pace. Excellent ones are listed on the next page and are available at local bookstores or online at amazon.com.

Check www.allbookstores.com for the print editions of the following books. They are listed for all bookstores around the country, cheapest price first. Dan Gookin, author of the Word titles, created the Dummies format with his original *DOS for Dummies* book in 1991.

Word 2010 for Dummies, by Dan Gookin
Paperback ISBN: 978-0470487723 $24.99

Word 2007 for Dummies, by Dan Gookin
Paperback ISBN: 978-0470036587 $21.99

Word 2003 for Dummies, by Dan Gookin
Paperback ISBN: 978-0764539824 $21.99

PowerPoint 2010 for Dummies, by Doug Lowe
Paperback ISBN: 978-0470487655 $24.99

PowerPoint 2007 for Dummies, by Doug Lowe
Paperback ISBN: 978-0470040591 $21.99

PowerPoint 2003 for Dummies, by Doug Lowe
Paperback ISBN: 978-0764539084 $21.99

Excel 2010 for Dummies, by Greg Harvey
Paperback ISBN: 978-0470489536 $24.99

Excel 2007 for Dummies, by Greg Harvey
Paperback ISBN: 978-0470037379 $21.99

Excel 2003 for Dummies, by Greg Harvey
Paperback ISBN: 978-0764537561 $21.99

New editions of these titles and Kindle editions are available at www. amazon.com.

Secret #4:

Use Accounting Software

"Using accounting software saves hours of time...because it reduces or eliminates redundant data entry...."

— Shelley Elmblad

Secret #4:
Use Accounting Software

Never send handwritten receipts or invoices. If you are at a trade show or other event where computer access isn't available, use preprinted order forms. A great source at reasonable cost is 5 Day Business Forms (www.5daybf.com).

To generate your documents at your office, use a quality accounting program, such as Quickbooks Pro. Quickbooks Pro is designed for the small business owner who has no accounting background. The setup is easy, and you can manage your business efficiently no matter what your industry or growth level is.

You can accurately track:

- product inventory
- payments from customers
- outstanding invoices
- bank account deposits and debits
- job costing
- income/expenses
- credits
- sales taxes
- customer records
- vendor list
- billable time

- performance trends
- payroll records

You can also generate:

- invoices
- credit memos
- profit and loss statements and other tax-related documents
- payroll records
- paychecks
- forms
- budgets
- business plans
- fiscal reports
- customized financial reports

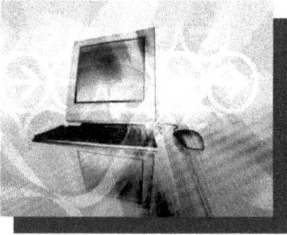

With this drag-and-drop software, you can also export files to Excel, attach receipts and other documents to invoices and customers files, and track sales leads.

Your accountant will appreciate those tax statements at tax time. Instead of handing him/her a virtual mountain of paper to wade through, you will be able to provide just a few sheets with everything itemized for easy processing. You'll save money on your accounting fees, too.

Secret #5: Brand Your Company and Your Products

"Your...brand had better be delivering something special, or it's not going to get the business."

— Warren Buffett

Secret #5:
Brand Your Company and Your Products

To attract top clients, your company must have a recognizable image. That includes your company name, logo, unique selling proposition, tagline, and marketing materials. These make up your brand.

An effective brand tells your prospects and customers who you are, what you do, and how you do it. It establishes your credibility. Your brand is how they perceive you, your company, and your products and services. Disneyland's brand, for example, is fun, wholesome, family entertainment.

Nick Usborne[2], web-writing expert, advises staying close to your passions. Prospective clients/customers will love to hear you speak and write with genuine enthusiasm about what you love.

Your brand should set your company apart from your competition. It should have four elements:

1. *Purpose*

What do you provide your customers? What traits do you want your company/products/services to be known for? For example, Starbucks is known for upscale coffee, not just coffee. Trader Joe's is known for healthy foods.

2. *Differences*

What can you/your company do that your competition can't? Promote this element in all of your marketing collateral. Take FedEx. This company is known for delivering packages overnight anywhere in the world. Few companies can say that.

3. *Personality*

What traits describe your brand? Nike's products, for example, are "young and hip." Crystal Light describes itself as sassy, vibrant, and fun. Does your company want to be known for being conservative? cutting edge? user-friendly? caring?

4. *Promise*

What is the promise you make to your customers? High quality? Great customer service? Reliability? Outstanding training? Next-day shipping? Promise value on the unique qualities your customers and clients want and need and that you can offer.

List the benefits you provide and anything else that sets you apart. The idea is to increase your prospects' awareness of your brand, business name, and logo, in addition to your products and services.

Karen Southall Watts[3], a consultant for new businesses, suggests remembering storytelling techniques. "Great stories have conflict—your customer's problem," she says. "Be the hero with a well-thought-out solution that proves you really know your audience."

Your Company Name

Your company name should describe exactly what your business does. While it may be tempting to have a whimsical name, such as "Butterflies and Rainbows," avoid it. This name might be cute, but it doesn't tell your customers what you do.

Let's look at some vague company names. Take the Smart and Final Iris Company (now known as Smart and Final). Would you know what this company does? It is not a flower shop. Smart and Final are the last names of the two male owners and Iris is the first name of the former female owner. This company is actually a non-membership warehouse grocery provider. How about Joe's Garage? No, it's not an auto repair place. It is an event venue featuring a classic car decor. You can see the importance of having a descriptive name. Here are some examples that work:

PetsMart	Toyota Motor Corporation
Kraft Foods, Inc.	Hallmark Cards
Famous Footwear	California Bank & Trust

Is there any doubt what these companies do?

Picking a name that suggests a large company can work wonders. Take U. S. Robotics, which makes high-performance modems. If this name conjures up the image of a giant megacorporation, that's exactly what founder Casey Cowell wanted his target market to think.[4] "My partners and I wanted a name that implied size, age, and power," he says. In reality, they originally ran this company from Cowell's kitchen table.

In addition, ensure your company name is unique and not similar to others in your area.

Your Logo

Your logo is your primary company image, and it should clearly represent the message your brand conveys. Using clipart or a stock logo from the local copy shop may be easier, but don't do it!

Brand your company and products with a distinctive image. Investing in a professionally designed logo is a must if you want to look like a Fortune 500 company.

Look at the logos below. Can you recognize the businesses that they represent?

Superman	AT&T	Nike	VolksWagon
Target	Apple	Mercedes	MasterCard
Toyota	Starbucks	Microsoft	McDonald's

Answers:

That's what you should go for: an identity that is clearly your company and no other. Find a graphic artist on www.guru.com or www.elance.com or get a recommendation from other businesses in your city.

Your Unique Selling Proposition

Why should a customer come to your small business rather than to one of your competitors? You must have something that sets you apart from those other businesses. What is it about your company that makes it the one clients should seek out? This is your unique selling proposition (USP).

Let's consider FedEx again. FedEx's USP is guaranteed overnight delivery. It's the one thing they do that most other delivery companies cannot. Your USP:

- drives your business success

- can be used as a branding tool

Interactive Marketing, Inc.[5], suggests that your company's USP can be broken down this way:

1. *Unique*

It clearly sets you apart from your competition, positioning you as the more logical choice.

2. *Selling*

It persuades a person to exchange money for a product or service.

3. *Proposition*

It is the offer and promise you make to your customer.

Alyssa Gregory[6], founder of the Small Business Bonfire, a social, educational, and collaboration community for entrepreneurs, suggests asking yourself these questions:

- What is the pain your target audience is feeling? Loss of customers? Financial problems? Relationship issues? How can your product or service solve that?

- What are the three main benefits of selecting your product or service to solve that pain?

- Why are these important to your target audience?

If you aren't sure what the answers are, survey your

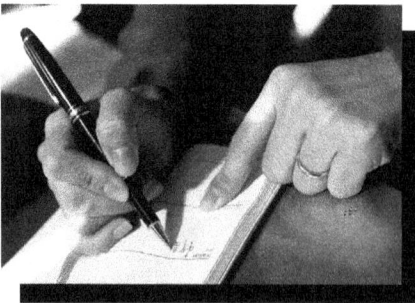

current customers. If you are just starting a business, survey people you hope to have as clients. The answers you receive should provide you with the data you need.

List all of this information on a piece of paper. One caveat: Don't promise what you can't deliver. If you do, you can ruin your reputation. Negative word of mouth spreads at a much more rapid rate than positive word of mouth.

So give some serious thought to your USP. It should be one clear phrase or sentence that creates a desire and an urgency for your clients or customers to buy.

Your Tagline

Like your logo and USP, your tagline should brand your company. And like your USP, this is a short phrase that describes what your company is known for. For example, Nike has the swoosh as its logo, but its tagline is "Just do it." Stargazer Publishing Company's is "Educate, Enlighten, Entertain."

Consider again FedEx's USP of guaranteed overnight delivery. Their tagline is "When it absolutely, positively has to be there overnight." Sometimes, your USP and tagline can have almost the same, if not the same, wording.

How many of the companies can you identify from these taglines?

"Don't leave home without it."

"We try harder."

"The quicker picker-upper."

The answers are below.

Answers: American Express, Avis, Bounty

Your Products and Services

Branding is all about trust. If you want your small business to be perceived at Fortune 500 company-level, your products and services must stand for quality and deliver the promises stated in your advertising and marketing materials. This means your company must have good quality control procedures for anything that goes out to your customers. The quality of your products and services shouldn't just meet or slightly surpass those of your competitors to win first place in the minds of potential customers; they must greatly surpass them. The workmanship must be impeccable. You don't want customers asking for their money back, but if they do, find out why. Fix any problems immediately and thank the customers for bringing the issue(s) to your attention.

Your products should carry your logo in color and your tagline. Use your products and services to push your brand and your brand to push your products and services. Get media coverage (e.g., Internet, radio, newspaper) to push brand awareness.

On your website, post the following:

- testimonials from your clients

- high-profile clients with whom you've worked

- awards you have received

- any community service with which your company has been involved.

Dave Dolak[7], a branding professional and author on branding issues, emphasizes that a strong brand can command premium pricing and signals that you want to create customer loyalty, not just sell a product.

Your brand, logo, tagline, and USP should be reflected in all your marketing materials, including your letterhead, envelopes, flyers, brochures, newsletters, postcards, order forms, business cards, website, social media sites, etc. Your message should be consistent through all of these elements.

To learn more about branding, check out the following resources:

Branding Basics for Small Business: How to Create an Irresistible Brand on Any Budget, by Maria Ross (2010) ISBN: 9781935254249 $15.95
Kindle edition $7.99

Smarter Branding Without Breaking the Bank: Five Proven Strategies You Can Use Right Now to Build Your Business at Little or No Cost, by Brenda Bence (2011)
ISBN: 9780982535318 $24.95
Kindle edition $9.99

Branding Your Business: Promote Your Business, Attract Customers and Build Your Brand Through the Power of Emotion, by James Hammond (2011)
ISBN: 9780749462963 $26.75
Kindle edition $14.97

The Old Rules of Marketing are Dead: 6 New Rules to Reinvent Your Brand and Reignite Your Business by Timothy R. Pearson (2011)
ISBN: 978-0071788229 $18.00
Kindle edition $9.00

Really Good Packaging Explained: Top Design Professionals Critique 300 Package Designs and Explain What Makes Them Work, by Rob Wallace, Bronwen Edwards, Marianne Klimchuk, and Sharon Werner (2009)
ISBN: 9781592535453 $45.00
Kindle edition $27.00

To purchase the hardcopies of these books at less than retail price, check the following websites:

- www.allbookstores.com

- www.amazon. com

Kindle editions, of course, are available only on Amazon.

Secret #6:

Develop Top-Notch Marketing Materials

"Your customers must be constantly educated about the many advantages of doing business with you...."

— Robert G. Allen

Secret #6:
Develop Top-Notch Marketing Materials

Hire a professional graphic artist to design your marketing collateral. Layout, proper use of white space, and writing ad copy that sizzles are crafts. Poorly designed materials will not help you; instead, they can damage your credibility.

If you have good graphics skills, use a page layout program with templates, like Microsoft Publisher, or a high-end page layout program, like InDesign, to create your brochures and flyers. Take a look at other companies' materials to get ideas. If you are marketing yourself instead of, or in addition to, your company, include a professional-looking headshot.

Another low-cost alternative is the graphics arts department at a local college or university. Ask for recommendations of students or professors who do quality work. You may be able to get a student to work for free or at low cost as an intern for college credit.

"I found an excellent graphic designer who works at very reasonable rates," says John Morales, who owns a car detailing business. "He was referred by a local printer, and he's given my company an image that others envy. People think we spent thousands on our logo, postcard design, and website banner. The truth is, we spent only hundreds."

If your company needs letterhead and envelopes, print them on quality paper, not on the plain bond meant for your laser or inkjet printer. Check with local printers, copy shops, office-supply stores, and online printing companies to get a good price. In addition, your brochure, letterhead, envelopes, business cards, mailing labels, flyers, and website should have a uniform look.

Secret #7:

Create a Major Internet Presence

"An effective web presence allows your company to be open 24 x 7, have a global audience, and present a professional and credible image."

— Global Commerce & Communication, Inc.

Secret #7:
Create a Major Internet Presence

Potential customers expect you to be on the Internet. Your company website is the first marketing element to develop, and it should have its own domain name (URL): your www.mybusiness.com address. Go to www.rickscheapdomains.com to register yours inexpensively. Create your website for free with free hosting at www.weebly.com.

Another user-friendly program for developing websites is Serif WebPlus. It comes with an impressive collection of terrific design templates, navigation bars, and graphics and works with the major shopping carts. Download a free trial version at www.serif.com. You'll need hosting.

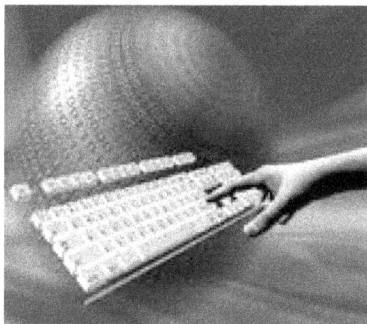

Wordpress is another good choice. Originally designed for blogs, it has evolved to handling full-fledged websites. While Wordpress itself is free, it is more difficult than Serif or Weebly to learn and use and you'll have to pay for hosting, but it has more versatility than Weebly. It is not WYSIWYG (what you see is what you get), however. If you are okay with not being able to see what you create until after it is created, you may do fine.

Wordpress and Weebly both have plug-ins for e-commerce via Paypal if you don't have a merchant account. If you do have a merchant account, Wordpress has plug-ins for www.1ShoppingCart.com, one of the most highly rated shopping carts. Marketing in the new millennium also requires you to have an active presence on social media sites, such as:

- Facebook
- LinkedIn
- Twitter

Create comprehensive business and professional profiles. Allow only colleagues and customers to post on your business-related sites. Also consider keeping a blog, but be aware that blogs need frequent updating. Refrain from posting photos of your family, vacations, etc., or information on personal topics on your business website, social media sites, or blog. Put all your web and social media addresses in your e-mail signature block.

For terrific home-study training and low-cost marketing strategies, go to Jessica Swanson's Shoestring Marketing Association at (https://shoestringmrktg. infusionsoft.com/go/SMK/cjamato/) and get your free Shoestring Marketing Kit. A great investment on this website is Jessica's Shoestring Marketing Bootcamp.

Another excellent option is Tom Antion's year-long, personalized, hands-on coaching program. Go to www.greatinternetmarketingtraining.com/

Secret #8:

Maintain a Professional Image

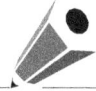

"Your appearance, attitude, reputation, and how you treat others play a tremendous role in contributing to your overall image and ultimate success."

— Joel D. Great

Secret #8: Maintain a Professional Image

When you are in your office, consider several aspects: your address, telephone, fax service, 800 number, office hours, website, social media sites, dressing for success, and meeting clients.

Address

Maintain a separate address for your company; don't use your home address. If you work from home, you don't want to risk prospects driving to your office unless you intend for them to do so.

Rent a PO box from the post office or a mail stop. One in a swanky area from a service that will forward your mail to your home is ideal. If this isn't possible, you can still rent a PO box or mail stop box in most towns.

The advantage of a PO box from the post office is that the post office lobby is open 24 x 7, so you can retrieve your mail whenever it is convenient. The advantage of the mail stop is that you can also use its physical address to make it appear as though you have a brick-and-mortar location. The downside is that mail stops are open roughly 8-6 and closed on Sundays. If you have to retrieve your mail in the off hours, you are out of luck. Another caveat is that prospects or customers may try to seek out this physical location expecting to find your office. Some customers may be put off that you don't have a real storefront.

Telephone

If you work from home, install a separate line for your business. Include a professional message with your business hours. Answer your phone with your company name. Do not allow your children, or anyone else not connected to your company, to answer this phone. Conduct business calls in a quiet environment away from noisy kids, barking dogs, TVs, radios, loud music, and other interferences. Return calls promptly. If you have customers out of your area code, arrange for an 800 number so they won't incur long-distance charges.

Fax Machine

Your clients may want to fax you information. Buy a standalone fax machine or a program through which you can receive faxes on your computer. A standalone fax machine will allow you to fax material that is not on your computer; faxing that material will otherwise require scanning first.

Office Hours

Maintain regular office hours during which your clients or customers can reach you. If you have a landline and will be out of the office for long periods of time, forward your calls to your cell phone or consider getting voice mail service from the phone company. Voice mail service allows you to access your messages remotely.

Website

This has been mentioned before, but it bears repeating. Every business worth its salt needs a website. Potential clients will expect the ability to check you out, along with your products and/or services, and the website is the way for them to do that.

Social Media Sites

This has been mentioned before, too, but it also bears repeating. The image you project online will reflect how your clients perceive you. Ensure that your social networking sites reflect only your professional image and background. You don't necessarily know what a potential client's likes and dislikes are. You don't want to lose business because you've offended someone or turned off him/her.

Dress for Success

Your image extends beyond your office to you yourself. You will be judged by what you wear. When meeting clients or customers, dress appropriately.

Casual clothes are fine if you are walking around a construction site or gathering on the golf course, but when meeting someone from the corporate world during working hours, dress in conservative business attire. Wear dress shoes.

In either case, be well-groomed, with cleaned and trimmed fingernails. Cover any tattoos or piercings, other than women's earrings. Women should wear minimal jewelry to prevent distracting jangles. Both men and women should avoid overuse of cologne or perfume since some people are sensitive.

"I hired a consultant to develop some brochures," says Joan Randall, Vice-President of a mid-sized marketing firm. "I had spoken to him only on the phone. His skills and the samples he had on his website were excellent, so I didn't think it would be a problem. When he came into the office, however, he had rings through his nose and ears, and tattoos on his neck and arms. In addition, he was wearing old jeans and a t-shirt. I had to unhire him—fast—since he would have to meet with our very conservative clients, and his image would reflect poorly on us."

Don't lose business because your image isn't what it should be.

Meeting Clients

Perhaps you meet regularly with clients who want to come to your office. If you have a physical building, this isn't an issue. If you work from home but don't want clients coming there, consider renting space as needed in an executive office building.

"I'm the sole proprietor of an advertising agency," says Terry Adams. "Clients regularly want to come to my office. I work from home, so I rent a conference room in a nearby executive suite whenever I need to hold meetings. My office phone goes through their switchboard when I'm not in. I can rent an office there, too."

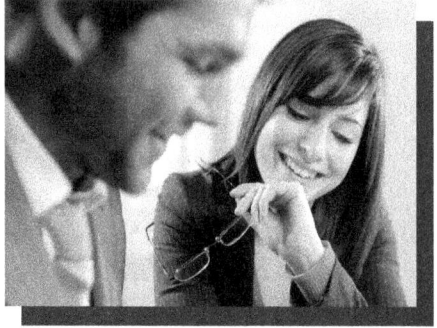

Other amenities include, but are not limited to:

- Breakroom

- Video conference room equipment

- Training rooms

- Fax/copy/scan/email access

- Computer equipment

- USPS/FedEx/UPS dropoff and pick-up services

- In-house postage meter services

- Client Service time (this gives the opportunity for tenants to temporarily "hire" executive office staff to assist with projects/assignments)

- Custom company signage

Search "executive suites" online or look in the Yellow Pages to find rentable space in your area.

An alternative is to rent the use of a conference room or office as needed in the space of another company. With the downturn in the economy, some organizations may have extra facilities they are no longer using. They may be just as happy to have you there as you are to have use of the space.

Secret #9:

Show Up On Time for Meetings

"When you are on time, you enhance your brand. When you are late, you devalue your brand. Being on time is a choice."

— Todd Smith

Secret #9:
Show Up on Time for Meetings

Nothing destroys a businessperson's credibility faster than not showing up on time for an appointment. Routinely arrive 5 or 10 minutes early.

If you have never been to the client's site, consider driving there the day before a meeting so you will know the way and the time needed to get there.

In addition, call the day before to verify. Emergencies arise; people are called away on business trips or have other issues come up. Save yourself a wasted trip; let your customers know you haven't forgotten the appointment or had an emergency yourself.

If a problem does arise, don't wait until the day before the appointment to let your client or customer know. Call immediately. This demonstrates that you value his or her time.

"I was scheduled to give a workshop at a company only thirty minutes from my office," says Caren Allen, a CPA for small business owners. "Southern California traffic is notoriously horrible. Because I couldn't predict how the traffic would be, I decided to go the night before and stay overnight in a motel. It was a good thing I did, because the freeway I took was shut down the next morning with an overturned big rig. Had I gone the morning of the workshop, I definitely would have been hours late."

Err on the side of caution; never keep your customers waiting.

Secret #10:

Charge Competitive Fees

"Don't undercharge your services. Remember, you are providing the expertise that your client needs and is willing to pay for."

— Andréa Coutu

Secret #10:
Charge Competitive Fees

If you are selling services, don't shortchange yourself with low fees. Charge what is competitive or only slightly below. Just because your business may be new doesn't mean you shouldn't be paid what you're worth. For your clients or customers, it's all about perceived value. If your rates are too low, you won't be taken seriously. Be competitive and you'll be level with counterparts who have been in business for years.

Where you live and the type of business you have will determine the rates you charge. If your competitors are local, look them up in the phone book or on the Internet. Check their websites to see if their fee schedules are posted. If not, call anonymously to find out their rates.

On the other hand, if your business competes with companies overseas in countries that charge half of what you do, you certainly can't and don't want to lower your rates to match theirs. Instead, make it your mission to convince your clients that it's worth paying the higher rates to have a source that is local and available whenever they need help.

Pam Newman[8] is a Certified Management Accountant and president of RPPC, Inc. This company provides customized business development services. Newman and www.geekpreneur.com[9] suggests asking yourself these questions before setting your fees:

- What are the direct costs of your product or service (materials and labor)?

- What are your business's indirect (overhead) expenses?

- What is your break-even point (costs and income are equal; no profit)?

- How is your competition pricing their offerings? (Don't just look at price. See how you can add value without adding costs.)

- What is the current state of your industry and the economy?

Some businesspeople look at the quality of their products and services and consider the competition on a global scale. If the quality you offer is truly world-class—and hard to find anywhere in the world—feel free to charge the highest rates a buyer is willing to pay.[10]

Newman adds that "every pricing decision you make should offer a win/win outcome where your customers get good value for their money and your business makes a reasonable profit."[11]

Don't underprice yourself!

Secret #11:

Perform Needs Assessments

"A needs assessment will help you determine whether your proposed work is truly necessary."

— Roger Kaufman

Secret #11:
Perform Needs Assessments

If you are selling services, set up an initial meeting with a potential client to assess the company's needs. Your client has a problem that must be remedied. Your aim is to understand that problem and show how you can solve it according to that client's requirements and budget. It isn't to twist your clients' wishes to fit your knowledge base.

Often, what the customer thinks are the problems are not really the problems at all but merely the symptoms of larger, unrecognized issues. It's up to you to interview as many people in the organization as you can to determine their perspectives. You will have to convince the customer of the importance of doing so. Only then can you discover those hidden issues.

"We wanted our website revamped," said Janice Peterson, the owner of a small consulting company. "We wanted to keep our current main page background in addition to our shopping cart, since it has autoresponders, affiliate programs, and contact management. It is the most highly rated shopping cart in the country.

"We spoke to two different programmers who wanted us to dump everything and allow them to recreate our website from scratch. This would have cost tens of thousands more than we had budgeted. Why should we pay to reinvent the wheel just because the programmers are unwilling to learn about and integrate our shopping cart? We didn't hire either of them."

Take a cue from the business owner's comments in the sidebar on the previous page. Meet your clients' needs, even if it means a learning curve on your part. Solving their problems is the first priority, and if you're willing to go the extra mile, you will be a first choice.

Secret #12:

Join Professional Associations

"Professional [associations] offer mentors, insight into how the industry works and how to navigate it, [and] professional development courses."

— Lauren Bayne Anderson

Secret #12:
Join Professional Associations

Membership in professional associations is a hallmark of being at the top of your game. While you may feel that you don't have the time, rethink your position. The benefits are numerous:

- Networking with others in your field

- Garnering referrals to other clients

- Keeping up with industry trends

- Seeing what your competitors are doing

- Increasing awareness of your company and its products or services

Put the associations' logos on your business card and website. You can also include links to their sites, if appropriate.

Find out the names of the key players and collect their cards and e-mail addresses. Write notes on the back of the cards so you remember who they are. Ask questions that will give you an excuse to contact them later. Also ask if you can add them to your database. Find ways to keep in touch; for example, getting on a committee is one way to hobnob without being obvious.

Those colleagues may refer you to prospects you could not have reached otherwise. You can also write articles for the association newsletter to raise awareness of your company on a broader scale.

Secret #13:

Follow Up on Leads and Contacts

"Follow-up isn't just about selling. It's about building relationships and allowing the sale to happen."

— Adrienne Zoble

Secret #13:
Follow Up on Leads and Contacts

The National Association of Sales Executives has discovered that 81% of all sales happen on or after the fifth contact.[12] Yet, according to David Frey, President of Marketing Best Practices, one important element 90% of business owners overlook after meeting with potential customers is follow up.[13]

Why?

Reasons include not wanting to appear pushy, being too busy or forgetful, and avoiding prospects who have not actually purchased.

The truth is that you won't seem pushy by being courteous, and being too busy or forgetful are not legitimate excuses. Neglecting to interact with prospects who are not yet customers leaves room for other businesses to gain the competitive edge. In addition, even if prospects aren't ready to buy your product or service, they could refer you to someone who is. That is valuable. Follow up on hot prospects you wish to cultivate. Think of it this way: You are laying the groundwork for them to purchase at a later date.

The first contact after your initial meeting should be a thank you note. Send one—whether or not you have sold the customer your product or service. Avoid sending an e-mail thank you; it may seem old-fashioned, but a snail-mail thank you makes a terrific positive impression. Even if the business relationship doesn't work out right away, there's always a chance in the future.

Send your thank you note within a day or two of your meeting. Keep it brief. Thank your prospect for taking the time out of his or her busy schedule to meet with you and state that you hope to do business together. Avoid any selling.

Your note can be handwritten or produced on your computer. Howard Olsen, the president of High Output Training Systems in Vancouver, B.C., says, "I created... a standard template...using MS Publisher.... I selected a handwriting font to make it personal.... [After] a meeting, I...open the document, make...slight modifications, print it, fold it, and stuff it into an envelope."[14] Customers love this extra effort.

Once you have sent your initial thank you note, there is no need to phone. E-mail, an autoresponder, or snail mail is better as it's less intrusive. Include something that will be of interest, such as a link to an interesting website or a copy of/link to a relevant article.

And what about follow-up after you have made the sale? This is also crucial to the success of your business relationship and the image of your company. Dan Ralphs, Business Development Manager at Infusionsoft, which sells an all-in-one sales and marketing software solution for small businesses, describes the typical customer lifecycle this way:

1. Generate interest
2. Sell to hot leads
3. Get new customer
4. Sigh in relief
5. Start over

This cycle is a big mistake, he points out. Your customer and lead database is a goldmine. Why have to reinvent the wheel when you can get repeat business from previous customers just by following up?[14]

Set up a system. Every so many days or weeks, check in with your list. Set aside a specific time to make or return calls or send emails. You want to ensure that everything is going well with your product or service and that the customers or clients are happy. Remind them what a great decision they made in purchasing from you. In addition, you want to convince them not only to buy from you again but also to recommend you to other potential clients or customers. Keeping your name fresh in their minds helps to maintain the trust you worked so hard to build and to ensure that you will be the one they will call when they need another product or more of your service or are asked for a referral.

Once you get the cycle going, automate it as much as possible so your customers don't slip through the cracks. This is where having an autoresponder system is critical; however, it is not a substitute for a personal call once in a while to let them know there is still a human being at your end.

Be proactive. Maintaining an organized database of leads and following up regularly will keep your business fresh in the minds of customers, close more sales, and make you thousands of dollars by putting you head and shoulders above your competition.

Secret #14:

Exhibit at Trade Shows

"Trade shows can catapult your business to success...[and are] a golden opportunity to meet the people you need to meet."

— Maria Brophy

Secret #14:
Exhibit at Trade Shows

Exhibiting at trade shows in your industry is a major way of getting your small business recognition and meeting potential clients or customers face-to-face. Some major benefits are as follows:

• Regional/National Exposure

Exhibiting allows you access to a large audience of new customers that you otherwise may not reach.

• Credibility

Buyers often say that they perceive business owners who exhibit as more credible than those who don't. While this may be an unfair assumption, the professional image of your business in a well-designed booth goes a long way to generating consumer confidence.

• Industry Awareness

Exhibiting at trade shows can also help you improve and keep up your expertise in your field, since you will see what your competitors have to offer.

• Face-to-face Contact

Current and potential customers can see the face behind the name. While online marketing should be an integral part of your marketing plan, a handshake goes far beyond your online presence. Cultivating face-to-face relationships with your prospects increases their confidence in your work.

• Networking

Trade shows provide a fantastic opportunity to meet exhibitors, vendors, wholesalers, and others in your field from around the country. Collect business cards. Ask permission to add them to your database.

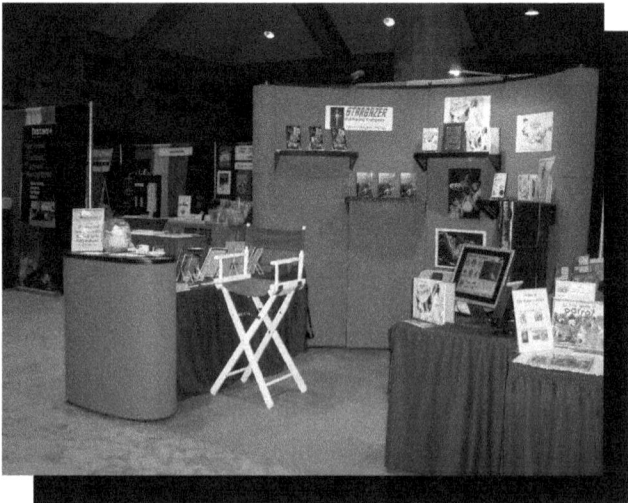

• Knowledge of Your Competition

Trade shows provide you the opportunity to see what other business owners are doing with their product presentations and marketing efforts.

• Impulse Orders

Be sure to allow attendees to handle your products or see handouts explaining your services. Offering your products or services at a "show only" discount creates an urgency for them to purchase. In addition, they don't have to pay shipping for physical goods.

• Speaking Opportunities

Think about offering to present at trade shows. The exposure for you and your company is well worth it. You could conduct a workshop, do a product demonstration, or be part of a panel. These arrangements are usually made a year in advance of each show, so get yourself on the program as soon as possible. Call the sponsoring organizations to find out who the program chair is. This person can give you all the details on the types of presentations the organization is seeking and the time lengths.

- ## Long-term Profits

  While some prospects may not buy your products or services right away, add them to your database (with their permission, of course) and keep them informed. The relationship you have created often encourages them to buy at a later date. They may become your most consistent buyers.

For economical ideas on exhibiting at trade shows, pre-order my book, *Maximize Your Visibility: Exhibiting at Trade Shows on a Shoestring Budget*, due out in 2015. See page 125 for more details. Call (800) 606-7895 or e-mail info@topwritingcoach.com for more information.

- Carol J. Amato
Top Writing Coach

Secret #15: Package Your Products in a Distinctive Manner

"Innovative packaging is an effective, powerful path to break through the sea of choices consumers face."

— Brand Zone

Secret #15: Package Your Products in a Distinctive Manner

We are a packaging-driven society. Sometimes, buyers are attracted more by the box something comes in than by the goods themselves. Your products, whether physical or digital, should have distinctive packaging. Physical items should be packaged well for safety during shipping.

Visual Appearance

Ensure that your physical products are in containers that:

- carry your logo
- explain the product's features, benefits, and requirements
- are visually appealing

The colors should match those on your marketing collateral. This reflects competitiveness and planning and will pique your customers' interest. Use preprinted shipping labels with your company name, address, and logo.

Your digital products should have cover pages and ad copy that meet these same requirements. Give them a uniform look; for example, use the same cover page format on proposals, special reports, or other short documents. Include your logo. Use the same fonts and layout not only on the cover but also on the interior pages. The same applies to any e-books (or other digital documents/products) or workbooks that you create.

Safety During Shipping

Think about keeping your physical products safe during shipping. You want them to arrive in perfect condition. Improper packaging is a sign of poor quality control, and that's not the image you want to project to your customers. Great packaging also helps you; you can spot your products easily on a shelf for inventory purposes.

Secret #16:

Develop Good Project Management Skills

"Every...organization's success depends on the strength of its leadership."

— Villanova University website

Secret #16:
Develop Good Project Management Skills

Consultants are often called upon to manage projects for their clients. Small business owners frequently manage projects within their own companies. Make sure your skills are up to the task:

- Know how to work with/direct a team.

- Be familiar with the four basic personality styles so you can use everyone's skills to the best advantage. Administer a personality test, such as the DiSC profile (www.onlinediscprofile.com, $25) or the True Colors test (www.true-colors.com, $34.95) to see what types you and your team members are. One important fact to remember is that there is no one "right" personality type. Each has its value and strengths.

- Assess the team members' strengths and weaknesses and delegate tasks accordingly.

- Know how to manage the following:

    - Scope (project size and goals)

    - Resources (people, equipment, material)

- Time (duration of specific tasks and the project as a whole, including allowances for unforeseen events)

- Money (costs and profit, including allowances for unforeseen costs)

• Write progress reports on a predetermined timeline to keep your client informed.

Secret #17:

Write a Book

"When you author a book addressing some facet of your industry, you become an authority and expert within that industry."

— Roger Killen

Secret #17: Write a Book

D o you want to impress your clients and be the go-to person in your industry? Do you want to reduce or eliminate cold-calling and have clients come to you?

You have expertise to benefit your target market in written, besides verbal, form. Nothing spells "expert" like a book, and nothing impresses clients more than a businessperson who hands them one he/she has written. Being able to call yourself an author puts you in a league above other small business owners and entrepreneurs. Not many are taking this additional, lucrative step.

No doubt you have extensive knowledge in several areas of your industry. Putting your expertise into book or e-book form will:

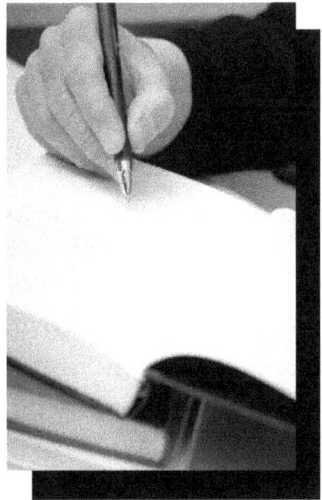

- position you as an expert

- gain you instant credibility

- widen your market to international level

- help you garner top-notch speaking opportunities

- attract a higher level of client

- create an additional stream of income

- draw media attention

You don't need to sell your book to a major publishing house anymore. You can self-publish it. You'll make all the profit. In addition, you can create additional information products from that same source material.

On the other hand, your book must still look as professional as one produced by a New York publisher. That means having a professionally designed cover and well-organized content that has been edited and proofread by pros.

Take as much time as you need to do a careful job. Good books aren't created overnight. Don't fall for the scammers who say you can write your book in three days or two weeks. You want to produce a book that your clients or customers and your industry will value.

Become the recognized expert in your market. Add that additional revenue stream. Write your book. Set aside a specific amount of time each day to write. Even an hour will do. Aim for at least 100 pages.

Worried about how to get started writing your book? Not sure how to organize your material? To achieve the goals of impressing your readers and making money, your book must be a quality product. For a step-by-step system from outlining to publication, go to p. 119 of this book and to my website, www.topwritingcoach.com, for information on my Write Your Way to Wealth Coaching program. You'll find all the help you need.

- Carol J. Amato
Top Writing Coach

The Bottom Line

"Advertise...something the competition doesn't have, something extra—icing on the cake."

— David Leonhardt

The Bottom Line

Standing out from your competition is critical to your success. Brand your business with quality. Give it a Fortune 500-company image to position yourself as an expert, attract more clients, and skyrocket your brand to the top.

"Specialize, be the expert, then deliver."

— Leigh Ann Otte

Endnotes

1. Bureau of Labor Statistics, http://www.bls.gov/bdm/entrepreneurship/entrepreneurship.htm

2. Nick Usborne, www.asknickusborne.com/article-building-your-brand.html

3. Karen Southhall Watts, http://www.namebranding authority.com/85-tips/

4. Carol J. Amato, "U.S. Robotics: Quality is Their Passion," *Communique*, November, 1988.

5. Interactive Marketing, www.interactivemarketing inc.com/unique-selling-proposition.html

6. Alyssa Gregory, http://www.sitepoint.com/how-to-create-unique-selling-proposition/

7. Dave Dolak, "Building a Strong Brand," http://www. davedolak.com/articles/dolak4.htm

8. Pam Newman, "Setting Competitive and Profitable Prices," http: //www.entrepreneur.com/article/167198

9. Geekpreneur, "Setting Competitive Rates Around the World," http://www.geekpreneur.com/setting-competitive-freelance-rates-around-the-world

10. Ibid.

11. Pam Newman, Ibid.

12. Dan Ralphs, Infusionsoft presentation at Author 101 conference, March 3, 2012, Los Angeles, California.

13. David Frey, "How to Win More Sales with Less Effort," http://www.businessknowhow.com/marketing/less_effort.htm

14. Howard Olsen, "The Perfect Followup," www.high-output.com/uncategorized/the-perfect-follow-up/, January 15, 2009.

15. Dan Ralphs, Ibid.

About the Author

Carol J. Amato, Top Writing Coach, has run her own business writing and training firm for over 25 years. She focuses on teaching business owners how to maintain a high-profile image through written communication. Her proven, step-by-step Write Your Way to Wealth system shows small business owners and entrepreneurs how to put their expertise into book form so they can position themselves as experts, attract more clients, and skyrocket their businesses to the top of their industries.

She has published 26 books, over 175 articles, and two short stories. Her articles have appeared in national publications and she was a regular contributor to high-tech magazines such as *Smart Computing* and *PC Novice*. Carol also has been an editor for major publishers and several magazines and has appeared on radio and television shows.

Besides *Maximize Your Competitive Edge*, her recent commercial titles include *How to Start and Run a Writers' Critique Group,* and *The World's Easiest Guide to Using the APA*, 4th Edition. Upcoming are *The World's Easiest Guide to Using the APA, 5th Edition,* and *The World's Easiest Guide to Using the MLA, 2nd Edition.* Due out in 2015 is *Maximize Your Visibility: Exhibiting at Trade Shows on a Shoestring Budget.*

Ms. Amato has a B.A. from the University of Portland in Portland, Oregon, and an M.A. from California State University, Fullerton, California.

She is a member of the Writer's Club of Whittier, Inc., a professional writers' critique group, and past president of the Professional Writers of Orange County. She was a board member of the Orange County Section of the Independent Writers of Southern California from 1988-1993. She is also a member of three other critique groups.

She is listed in *Who's Who in the West, Who's Who in the America*, and the *World Who's Who of Women*. She lives in Southern California.

Additional Resources

The Ultimate Guide to Electronic Marketing for Small Business
by Tom Antion, 2005, John Wiley & Sons
ISBN: 978-0471718703 $19.95

How To Blog, Build An Audience And Kick-Start Your Brand or Business Without Selling Your Soul
by André Klein, 2011
Kindle edition $7.99

One Great Goal
by Ursula Mentjes, 2009, Potential Quest, Inc.
ISBN: 978-1934379745 (softcover) $20.00
Available from www.salescoachnow.com
Kindle edition $7.99

Selling With Intention
by Ursula Mentjes, 2011, Morgan-James Publishing
ISBN: 978-1600378416 (softcover) $16.95
      978-1600378423 (Kindle) $7.99

Words that Sell: More than 6000 Entries to Help You Promote Your Products, Services, and Ideas
by Richard Bayan, 2006, McGraw-Hill
ISBN: 978-0071467858 $16.95
Kindle edition $9.99

More Words That Sell
by Richard Bayan, 2003, McGraw-Hill
ISBN: 978-0071418539 $16.95
Kindle edition: $9.99

Phrases That Sell
by Edward Werz and Sally Germain, 1998
ISBN: 978-0809229772 $14.95
Kindle edition $9.46

The 7 Habits of Highly Successful People
by Stephen R. Covey, 2004, Free Press
ISBN: 978-0743272452 $30.00
Kindle edition $7.81

Blogging for Business
by Shel Holtz and Ted Demopoulos, 2006,
Kaplan Publishing
ISBN: 978-1419536458 $21.95

Social Media Marketing an Hour a Day
by Dave Evans, 2012, Wiley Publishing, Inc.
ISBN: 978-1118194492 $29.99
Kindle edition $16.49

New Rules for Customer Service
by Sophia Brooks, 2011,
ISBN: 978-1441508898 $24.95

Free Special Report!!

Attention
Small Business Owners
and Entrepreneurs!

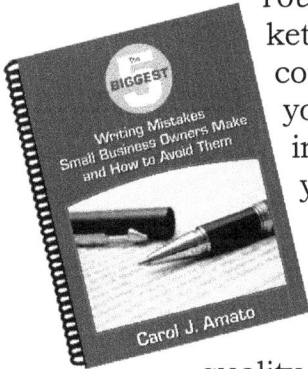

Your expertise is valuable to your market, but in today's tough economy, competition is stiff. The image that your small business projects in writing can determine if a client hires you or not. Whether you work from home as a solopreneur or have a brick-and-mortar location with employees makes no difference. You no doubt believe you provide quality to your customers, but do you find yourself asking these questions?:

- Why do my reports get ignored?

- Why do my proposals get rejected with no apparent reason?

- Why don't I get positive responses to the letters and emails I send?

- Why don't my marketing materials have an impact?

- Why am I struggling to break free from my competition?

- Why am I not the go-to person/company in my specialization?

The answer could be how your materials are written.

If you want to stand apart, your skills must be top-notch. They are the true public face of your business. Your writing is YOU. Your customers and clients will judge the quality of your products or services by the quality of your written communication. They will judge YOU by how you handle this skill set.

Go to www.topwritingcoach.com for your FREE copy of this informative special report. Get the inside scoop on the five biggest writing mistakes small business owners make and how to avoid them.

Business Writing Mastery
Home Study Program
Coming in 2015!

To begin your journey perfecting your business writing skills, I'd like to invite you to check out my Business Writing Mastery program. Just go to www.topwrit ingcoach.com/businesswriting mastery.

In this 5-module program, I will show you the secrets to writing five main types of business documents so that you can position yourself as an expert, attract more clients, and skyrocket your business to the top.

Each module takes you step-by-step through the process for writing that particular type of document. Rather than the information overload provided in one-day seminars, you get an in-depth explanation of each type and examples for each step accompanied by a transcript and workbook. Learn at your own pace. There's no need to move on to the next step until you are comfortable with the current one.

Through these modules and workbooks, you will learn:

- business writing basics
- how to use graphics effectively

and how to write:

- amazing reports
- proposals that win
- emails, letters, and memos that impress clients

Learn business writing the user-friendly way. To get on the mailing list so you'll be notified first when this program is available, e-mail info@topwritingcoach.com.

Write Your Way to Wealth
Coaching Program

Overwhelmed with the idea of writing a book? Not sure how to organize your material?

Do you want to be the go-to person in your industry? Do you want to reduce or eliminate cold-calling and have clients come to you?

Nothing impresses a client more than being handed a book (or books!) you've written. Being able to call yourself an author puts you in a league above other small business owners and entrepreneurs. Not many are taking this additional, lucrative step.

No doubt you have extensive knowledge in several areas of your industry. Putting your expertise into book or e-book form will:

- position you as an expert

- gain you instant credibility

- widen your market to an international level

- help you garner top-notch speaking opportunities

119

- create an additional stream of income

- draw media attention

Don't be overwhelmed by the idea of writing a book, but beware the scammers who say you can write one in three days or a few weeks. With my easy, step-by-step Write Your Way to Wealth system, you'll effortlessly write a *quality* nonfiction book through a combination of group and individual telecoaching and user-friendly instructions in transcript and workbook forms.

Among the many things you will learn are how to:

- develop a brand strategy with your book

- organize your information for maximum impact and usability

- create valuable information products from the same source material

- ensure your page layout is visually appealing

- publish your book in e-book and print forms

Your clients will be in awe at your results.

For more details, go to www.topwritingcoach.com/writeyourwaytowealth.html

What others say about Carol's coaching...

"I finished my manuscript [but] I had no clear idea how to present this book project to prospective publishers. With Carol's help, I learned how to query publishers and how to communicate with them in person. I got not only one publisher acceptance but two! I was able to choose the better fit for my book. Without her assistance, the process never would have gone as smoothly or as quickly. I am certain that her coaching helped me make the necessary connections with the publishers."

> *- Ann Camacho*
> *IB English Teacher*
> *John W. North High School*
> *Riverside, California*

"I would highly recommend Carol Amato without hesitation. Her expertise...is exceptional.... Above all else, Carol was a pleasure to work with. She was always...willing to go the extra mile. She knows the ins and outs of the business and was a great asset.... She is a consummate professional."

> *- Rhonda Fischer*
> *Award-winning author*
> Randy Kazandy
> *www.randykazandy.com*

"With Carol's guidance, I began to include educational teacher/study guides with each of my books. Since I began incorporating educational material with my manuscript suggestions, I've had five picture books accepted for publication."

> *- J. Aday Kennedy*
> *Freelance writer/author*
> *The Differently-Abled Writer*
> *www.jadaykennedy.com*

What others say about Carol's coaching...

"You have been a great [coach] and have given us a lot of material to take with us. It has been a pleasure being in this workshop."

- Tracy Godwin

"Carol is a great person to do business with. She's straightforward and honest, yet easy to work with. If you work with Carol, you can trust her to do the right thing, every time. I can't say that about most people."

- Dave Broughton
Marketing Consultant
WhimPublishing

"I have learned a tremendous amount of valuable information that I have immediately implemented at work and will continue to use in my future."

- Tony Soares

"Thanks...,Carol, for being such a great [coach] and being patient when I couldn't figure out how to get my words on the page right."

- Trudy Miller

What others say about Carol's coaching...

"Thanks...,Carol! I have taken two of your workshops now and I must say that I am always surprised at how well [they] flow. It has been great to have you as [a coach]."

- Jacklyn Couchman

"It was a pleasure to learn from you in this workshop. [It] was phenomenol and I could not have asked for an easier, more communicative session."

- Mia Sardarsingh

I have really learned a lot in writing and communicating effectively. I thank you for everything.

- Sheldon L. Bailey

"This has been the best workshop! It has made me more confident and much more valuable. Because of what I learned, I actually landed an amazing new job about three months ago."

- Dusty Crowell

"I cannot effectively express the wonderful, dramatic impact you have had on my life. You have awakened and fed a love for writing and the writing process that has been starving to death inside me. I will forever be grateful to you."

- Cyndi Rowland

"You gave this group the confidence and encouragement to strive toward their goals. You have been an outstanding coach. Thank you so much."

- Boaventura Muchanga

Maximize Your Visibility: Exhibiting at Trade Shows on a Shoestring Budget
(Due out 2015)

You've started your small business. Now you're faced with an even greater task: marketing. If you have been running your small business for years, you already know this. In this sluggish economy, however, how can you reach a large audience effectively?

One great way is to exhibit at trade shows, conferences, and conventions. Some major benefits are:

- Regional exposure
- Credibility
- Face-to-face contact
- Networking
- Industry awareness
- Knowledge of your competition
- Impulse orders
- Speaking opportunities
- Long-term profits

Exhibiting at local and regional trade shows doesn't require spending thousands. It can be done economically, yet fabulously, if the right steps are followed and the pitfalls are avoided. This guide will show you how.

ISBN: 9781933277172 (softcover) $14.95

Order Form

✓ Yes! Pre-order me the print version of

Maximize Your Visibility: Exhibiting at Trade Shows on a Shoestring Budget (due out 2015)!

Name _____

Address_____

City_____State_____ Zip_____

Email _____

Quantity _____ x $14.95 ea. $_____

Shipping/Handling $4.50 ea. $_____

Autograph it for me! $1.00 ea. $_____

CA sales tax 8.75% $_____

TOTAL $_____

MAIL TO:

Stargazer Publishing Company
PO Box 77002
Corona, CA 92877-0100

OR

Order online at www.topwritingcoach.com

OR

Call (800) 606-7895   Fax (951) 898-4633